Whispers Between the Lines

By Patricia A. Killingsworth

Copyright © 2011 Patricia A. Killingsworth.

All rights reserved. No part of this book may be used or reproduced by any means, graphic, electronic, or mechanical, including photocopying, recording, taping or by any information storage retrieval system without the written permission of the publisher except in the case of brief quotations embodied in critical articles and reviews.

ISBN: 978-1-4525-3735-1 (sc)
ISBN: 978-1-4525-3736-8 (e)
ISBN: 978-1-4525-3734-4 (hc)
Library of Congress Control Number: 2011913738

Balboa Press books may be ordered through booksellers or by contacting:

Balboa Press
A Division of Hay House
1663 Liberty Drive
Bloomington, IN 47403
www.balboapress.com
1-(877) 407-4847

Because of the dynamic nature of the Internet, any web addresses or links contained in this book may have changed since publication and may no longer be valid. The views expressed in this work are solely those of the author and do not necessarily reflect the views of the publisher, and the publisher hereby disclaims any responsibility for them.

The author of this book does not dispense medical advice or prescribe the use of any technique as a form of treatment for physical, emotional, or medical problems without the advice of a physician, either directly or indirectly. The intent of the author is only to offer information of a general nature to help you in your quest for emotional and spiritual well-being. In the event you use any of the information in this book for yourself, which is your constitutional right, the author and the publisher assume no responsibility for your actions.

Any people depicted in stock imagery provided by Thinkstock are models, and such images are being used for illustrative purposes only.
Certain stock imagery © Thinkstock.

Printed in the United States of America

Balboa Press rev. date: 8/18/2011

Acknowledgement

I'd like to give a special thanks to my husband and children as they have been, and continue to be, my strongest cheerleaders. There are many whom I would like to thank who have encouraged and supported me along the journey while creating this project. There are also several people who have been a divine source of inspiration, persons who do not even know me and to all of them I am grateful.

Table of Contents

                                                Page

Acknowledgement.. 2

Introduction.. 4

Preface.. 6

Chapter One
      Wee Whispers................................... 7

Chapter Two
      A Whisper of Hope........................... 12

Chapter Three
      A Whisper of Love............................ 69

Introduction

I have spent many years doodling and journaling, mostly for my benefit and enjoyment. These writings are a recounting of the journaling I have been doing since the early 90's. At times they were a release of emotion, other times they were pieces of my past, all things that were being revealed so that I could better work through them. Continuing to journal, and on occasion re-reading the journals, is when I started to see, really notice, some of the writings and phrasings were ringing true. *I was hearing whispers.* For some time I had realized that my doodling looked like Angels, *again the whispers.*

The decision to compile these works in the form of a book began shortly after loosing my mother and sister both from long term illnesses the previous year. It seemed that when the decision had been made, I couldn't get pen to paper fast enough! The more I wrote and worked with the Angels, the more excited I became about the project. When I looked back at those journals the *whispers* became more apparent.

I had noticed a shift that was quite significant at this time. I also realized the more I worked with the collection from my journals, there was a peace. My life was getting better, more serene; certain meanings to things were showing up bringing an actual balance in my life. Time usually is an issue with me, although, everything seemed to be getting done. There had to be something to all of this and I felt I needed to share it with others.

In reviewing my life, the journals, and the Angels that first showed up as just doodles, I saw that I used to ignore the *whispers*, perhaps because I felt *between the lines*.

Though I have worked as a free lance artist from time to time, I had never really considered myself a writer. It came to my awareness during this process, that a writer is merely someone who puts pen to paper; *more whispers*.

I kept these writings as they came to me. Some are in the form of guidance and some are more in the form of self-affirmations. I chose to keep them in the context in which they were written, as that is how I received their benefit. I can only hope the profound transformation I experienced while working on this project will be experienced by you as well. It really is my pleasure to share this gift, *the whispers,* with you all.

Today, I try to hear the *whispers* more. When I realize I may be once again, *between the lines,* it is a signal. I am probably in transition, as I believe is the World.

Preface

The Earth is changing and the pages you are about to read have the ability to help you in your life, as they have helped me in mine. I believe the messages are from the Angels, written over and over since the beginning of man's attempts to communicate. Words of wisdom, words of guidance, angelic forms of light; the time is now, the masses need to heal. They are timeless words of direction and encouragement. Open the pages and explore, open your heart to feel the love, open your mind to receive the guidance and the wisdom. Your days will be brighter. Your path will be illuminated as each step you take will be accompanied by the angelic light. May we all have the experience of connecting through love.

Wouldn't the world truly be a better place?

Each day an Angel to accompany you along your journey, each night an Angel to watch over and assist you on your slumber travels.

Enjoy………..

and spirit called

Chapter One

Wee Whispers

Friendship

Believing in yourself while in the midst of adversity and controversy, and to continue on your path without waiver, shows strength.

Delivering difficult messages, even though you know they won't be received well, takes courage.

There is a synchronicity in the universe; we can see it if we allow ourselves the time to look.

Find your passion, that which excites you, your truth and your soul's desire; there is no more time left to delay living.

Reflections of the past build the gateways of tomorrow.

Only by knowing where I have been will I be able to know where I am going.

I am aware each experience has a lesson associated with it.

As you enter into the realm of silence, there you will be able to see your attachments and let them go.

I am inspired when I am able to enjoy the simplicities of life.

Love

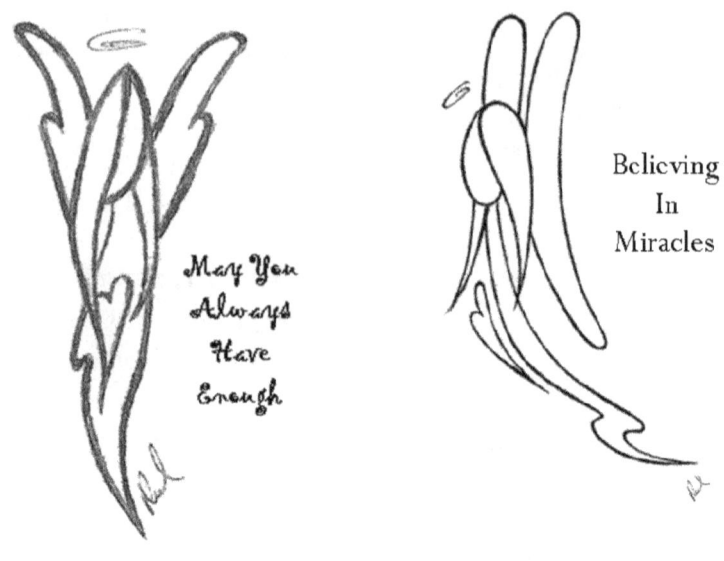

~Dream~

Know and trust the time has come to
manifest your new reality.

It is not what you seek, but
what you are open to receive.

The veil of illusion,
not one of deceit;
Listen not to my words,
but hear with my feet.

Dreams are the Gateway of Tomorrow

FOLLOW THE DRUM BEAT OF YOUR HEART

The person we are is a choice of what we hold on to and what we invite into our lives. What we attach ourselves to is what we become.

Life has been a series of lessons; the wisdom I have gotten as a result is what I reference as I venture forward onto my next experience.

Each step is so welcome, as I know those lessons are exactly what I need to have.

Chapter Two

A Whisper of Hope

There are times in life where the journey towards unification is the path one must travel alone. In a mindful trek paced by the rhythm of your heart and breath, you will begin to dance to the choreography of your soul. As the sacred ceremony of your soul reveals itself, the dance will naturally come to you. With each step you become closer to the source, at some point there is no separation. The realization is that there is only one, a symphony, a harmonious blend of souls embracing the knowledge that the source, at our core, we are one. Once you know, everything has changed, there is no turning back. The past as we knew it, good and bad, is a mere fading memory as we become awakened to the truth. There are many roads, though some are more direct than others. Every experience along the way is a necessary segment, none of which can be minimized even if the journey spans many lifetimes. There is no time frame in the universe as to when we as individuals hear our souls calling and begin the journey. The awakened soul, illuminated by the truth, the connection, the knowing, we are one.

and spirit called again

*B*elieve and make it so.

All things are possible…

In a world so filled with information, direction and opinion, I have found that my faith and a connection to the source is all I truly need.

*Illuminations
of love.*

Never are we truly
alone if we have
a heart.

That is where we are
all connected.

Only by giving will
you be able to
receive.

Embrace the possibilities as the universe knows no boundaries.

To give from the heart is love.

It is only then I am able to fully receive.

Simplicity is best.

Simplicity and self-validation are necessary if I am going to shine.

Mind
Body
and
Soul

There is no
separation
in one.

The area between reckless and sacred
is where I find the essence of my core.
There is great safety in my center and
access is by invitation only.

At some point we all experience the Great Merge, though with some of us it may not be so dramatic. This is where our past meets our present and they merge into what we call our future. These are notable times in our lives, the coming of age or when our life may take a sharp turn, some profound chain of events take us all to the Great Merge. I have been generously gifted with several of these experiences during my lifetime and they all have been a bit intense. I like to think I'm fairly carefree, though those around me may differ, but when I am at the threshold of a Great Merge I feel like I am being propelled by the force of every emotion, memory or belief I have ever had. There must be a great purpose for this, a universal time clock of sorts with a zero tolerance for being late. It keeps coming up and each time rings true that timing is everything and it is now.

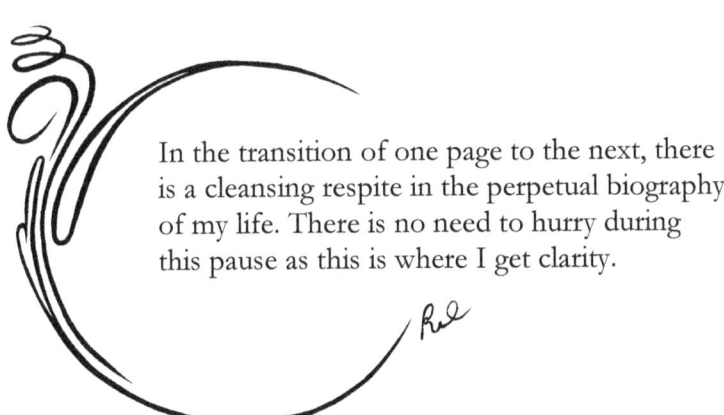

In the transition of one page to the next, there is a cleansing respite in the perpetual biography of my life. There is no need to hurry during this pause as this is where I get clarity.

Living as your authentic self.

From the depths of mystique movement is life.

Adapting is not surrender but acceptance.

Have the courage to explore the beyond.

There is nothing by chance, to be present and aware,
Listen to my inner knowing, it is love I am to share.
Open my heart and reach out a hand,
It is in a unified circle, strength in the band.
Shaking loose from the slumber, from days of old,
The shaking has released, it has been foretold.
The dark forces are banding in a desperate quest,
Be mindful, be present and love for the rest.
Power in numbers, as our gifts now awaken,
To help the masses and forgive the forsaken.
A release from the bondage of shame,
The past must stay past, without any blame.
We bring forth all our experiences, to the now and ahead,
Our circle, the power of love must be said.
Shine like a beacon, illuminate and shine,
For those who come after, you'll know from a sign.
It is as it has been told, the future is now,
Look for the guidance, you'll receive your how.
Divine light, the goodness, love enough for all,
Help is here for those who call.
Bring forth your gifts, the time is here,
Release any attachments of the past and your fear.
Faith and love, connection to the divine,
The long anticipated, forthcoming sign.
Love is the answer, love is the key,
Love is the truth that will set you free.

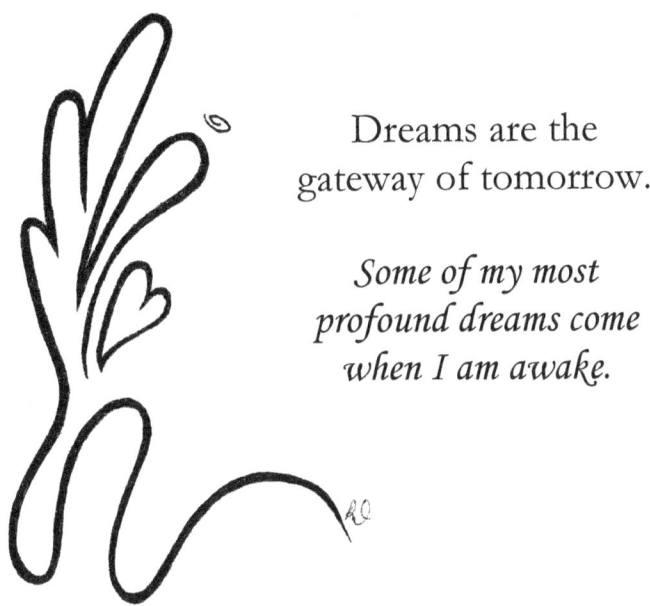

Dreams are the gateway of tomorrow.

Some of my most profound dreams come when I am awake.

A Matter of Choice

Sorrow and grief bring us to a place of opportunity, a time to grow and a time to let go. Redefine the importance and priorities in our lives. Shake it loose, as with any earth shattering experience, grief gives us the opportunity to cleanse; freedom from the bondage of our past, archaic beliefs, and outdated motives. What really is important anyway? When it comes right down to it, what really counts? When you are stripped of everything, what is left? You, your beliefs your character; what best serves, not only for you but those around you? Who we are is really stated by what we surround ourselves with. If you want to invite a calm and serene environment, you need to consciously step away from the "war zone." If you want to invite joy, you must step away from anger. If you want health, you must step away from dis-ease! So simple, yet our subconscious can hold us hostage because we let it.

Embracing the now,
timing is everything.

Life is a **choice**.

Don't confuse being alive with *living*.

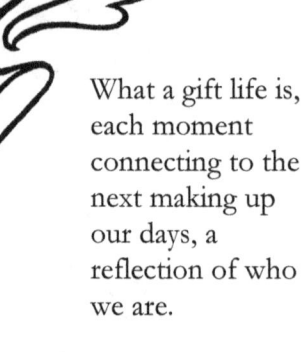

What a gift life is, each moment connecting to the next making up our days, a reflection of who we are.

Freedom in Forgiveness

To let down the barriers, the self imposed walls of fear I thought that I was protecting myself with. I found they were walls of imprisonment, filled with anger, judgments and resentments. Freedom was found when I courageously became vulnerable and humbly walked through those fears and allowed love back into my heart.

Each Day a Breath of a New Beginning

I know today I have choices; I no longer have to accept the unacceptable. I can redirect my life at any time, embracing each day, knowing that it brings about the threshold of my future.

See past the illusionary veil of deceit.

Things aren't always as they appear. Even in the darkest of times there is *Light*.

Dream into a new reality

Dream your new reality

~Dream~

When I am aware of the crisp
clear sound of silence,
I know I have connected,
I know we are one.

**Cherish the
Moments**
as they are only a
Skip in ***Time***.

From Near and Afar

To share with another…
Listen to the subtle whisper, the breath of the divine,
There you will hear the guidance, the future to unwind.
Above in the sky, the universal gifts,
Blessings so serene, no longer to drift.
Reach for the sky, my child, and you'll see,
The miracles and blessings are there and are free.
Far and so close, the truth that you seek,
The wisdom will help many, the strong and the meek.
Bring forth my child, the many gifts you bestow,
To help and to share for others to grow.
Come my child, alone you are not,
The gift and the blessing, abundance you've got!
Share and receive more than you give,
A bountiful life you'll see that you live.
The destiny you've been given, the time has arrived,
To come to the plate, for humanity survived.
The ugly, the dark, fear-based, distraught,
The healing will come, for many you'll have taught.
Blessings abound, the blessings you'll see,
Alive and awake, the masses set free.
Here you sit, alone and blessed,
Content with your blessing, truth that's confessed.
Be still my child, the universe will call,
For you to come, and join with them all.
There are many like you, friends to the core,
The blessings await, there are more in store.
Blessed and gifted, so special you are,
Many will seek you, from near and afar.
Love is the answer, love is the key,
The masses will heal in your lifetime you'll see.
The time has come, the divine gifts to call,
For you and the others, to respond and stand tall.
Blessed be my child, know you are loved,
From near and afar, from there and above.

Each Day
is a
New Beginning

As it ends and
so it begins

Where I go
and what I do
comes with the
Invitation
I allow myself to
receive from the
Heart

Courage to Change

Loosing the protective
armor...

Getting vulnerable does not
mean loosing control, but
putting the guard down.

As I observe, I find the
mirror effect to be very
healing. As I clearly see
the traits that no longer
serve, I am able to
freely let go and create
a vacuum for that
which I want to invite
into my life.

Only through the darkness will you see the light.

Something I never really understood until I had the privilege to experience a series of events in my life that brought me to that *dark place*. There it was revealed to me the magic of faith.

THE UNIVERSE HAS CALLED...

Deep in the depths of our soul, the core of our being, lays the chamber of secrets, knowledge and power of all our past. Lifetimes of experiences waiting to surface and blend with the life of our present existence. To acclimate our many lifetimes into one, a collection of many facets of the whole, now called upon as the universe sets in motion the playing field. Timing is everything and now is where we must be showing up completely, armed with all of our layers, completely able to emerge into this new earth that we have been co-creating for many lifetimes. Time and its entirety, time and eternity, time and all that is now present and being, now in the multifaceted realm. Life as it is in its morphing phase is like looking through a bug's eye, fractured and faceted, shifting perception of our narrow linear belief, the higher vibrational frequencies we are being asked to acclimate ourselves to. Bring forth the gifts that have been bestowed upon you. Bring forth the expanse of wisdom gathered and collected of your many lifetimes of existence. Bring forth and integrate yourself into the whole powerful being you have been destined to be in this incarnation. Shine and lead the way for so many seeking. Awaken to your true self. Shine brightly as your soul star pulses with the wisdom of the ages. Your powerful gifts are needed now, do not delay. Your physical needs and your worldly obligations are and will continue to be more than met. The universe has called and awaits your arrival.

Through our
vibrational being…..

Together we create the
Symphony
of **Life**

Whenever
I close my eyes
the **sky** is
always
Blue...

Illuminated By Grace

A shining star, so brightly seen,
Hope for many, twinkle and sheen.
The time has come, the earth may rise,
For the ancient treasures, so brilliantly wise.
Time is now, to wait no more,
There is no race, no keeping score.
We win by doing, by living with grace,
Guidance from divine, for the whole human race.
Sent to many, the messages come,
By pen, intuition, a knowing of some.
Blessed are the days, our future awaits,
All of mankind to fulfill their fates.
Excited and ready, as the new earth unfolds,
For all through the ages, the prophecies told.
Fear not my children, the time is now,
For faith has brought you, your lifetime somehow.
It is as it should be, the end of an age,
As the new now begins, like a turn of a page.
Bring forth my child your knowledge, your gifts,
As mankind awaits, no longer adrift.
Shine brightly my child, like a beacon in the night,
With hope and faith, with untold delight.
The time is now, we wait no more,
It is the beginning, just walk through the door.

How we
Respond
to the Life
we're **Given**,
is by the
Life we are
Choosing
to **Live**.

Enjoy the journey
as each step has its own destination
The timeless question of
"are we there yet"
comes to mind.
The answer quite simply is yes…

Peace
is a state of
Being

Love
is the
Answer

There are no
"buts"
in **Love**
or
Friendship

Being in the Now…

Timing is everything!

The Now reality is a concept that brings about hope.

I have realized that each moment, such as this moment, are precious and should be experienced to the fullest.

Seeking solution, every day,
Embracing those solutions that come my way.
The dawn is here, the new morn awaits,
With all to rise, and endure our fates.
Consequences for our choices and acts,
We rise to receive, the news like facts.
We are all here, at this time and alive,
To help one another, for the Earth to survive.
Coming together, there is no more time,
The unit of one, it is now a sign.
The Earth is the unit, we all make up,
The negative must go, the cruel and corrupt.
Peace and love are the call for the day,
As we each make a choice, to determine our way.
The time has come, the prophets say now,
What we must now do, is release and say how.
Join together in love and in peace,
Together is how, there will be a release.
Of the dark and the angry, fighting and greed,
No longer welcome, to satisfy our need.
Peace and love, that is our prayer,
To heal the masses and clear the air.
The time has come, foretold through the ages,
A time of reckoning, wrote by the sages.
Peace and Love, in a unified way,
The answers to all, who call out and pray.
Together as one, and know it is right,
Together to win, a stoppable fight.
As it once was, it will be again,
The end now the beginning, it starts from within.
Hope, there is plenty, enough for one and all,
With unity and prayer, together you call.
Love and Peace, the answer of truth,
To save the planet, for the innocent youth.
There is change world-wide, so many in fear,
It is through Love you will see, the air now clear.
The divine is here, to help and to heal,
Together is the answer, many will feel.
Together with Love, that is the key,
The planet transformed, soon it will be.
A planet of Peace, a planet of Love,
The answer is coming, from the divine place above.
Open you heart, release your fear,
Together with Love, hold close that which is dear.
Peace and Love will heal all that seems wrong,
You will see the change, to Love before long.
Release your fears, your troubles and strife,
And open your arms, to your newly found life.

~Together with Love~

Embracing
your
Authenticity

Authenticity
comes with
self realization.

Perfection without
question.

All is Well

Love is Always the Answer

the ***Magic*** of the ***Journey*** lies within each ***Step***

In the midst of adversity
There are blessing to be found
Be focused and see
The gifts that abound

Things never really
Are as they seem
Look past the obvious
To the clarity stream

Perception is everything
Detachment a must
So caught in the spin
You think you will bust

Exhale the toxins
The drama and strife
When you think you're at the end
You'll have found your true life

It's all there
For you to see
Amidst the chaos
The Will to be free

Free of the burdens
We carry and stow
Release the unnecessary
Soon we will know

Less is more or so
I've heard some say
The more I release
The better my day

The world of choice
And consequence too
The options are there
Good and bad, what to do

I choose the high road
To do the right thing
I know I've chosen well
When I hear my heart sing

Dreams do come *True*

What Defines Me?

I have had a variety of experiences in my life, and though my life has been affected by them, they do not define me.

What defines me is how I respond to those experiences.

What I do in life as a result of them; that is what defines me.

Each of our lives leaves an imprint, a personal legacy; that is what defines me.

The solution lies within...

Only there
in the depths
of your being
will you see the light.

The illumination of slumber
to your awakened state.

Heaven* and *Earth
merge into
a ***Harmonic***
vibrational *Melody*

Change is inevitable,
necessary for growth.

Awareness,
connection with spirit
and the gift of choice
are all so important.

What you do with them
makes all the difference.

We are all at the
doorway of opportunity…

It is up to all of us,
Individually,
to walk through and
graciously accept
what is being
gifted to us.

Breaking Free

Ridding myself
of
all that
no longer serves.

Love~Forgiveness
for giving *Love*.

Our *Hearts* sing
as one…

The *Melody* goes flat
when there is judgment.

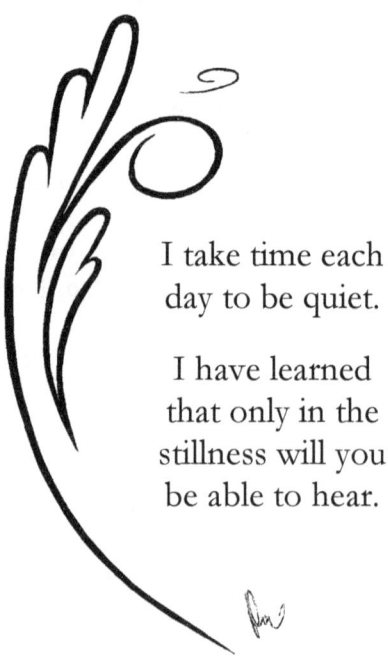

I take time each
day to be quiet.

I have learned
that only in the
stillness will you
be able to hear.

The more I let
go the more I
receive…

I freely and
generously
share the
abundance I
am graced
with, knowing
that there is an
infinite supply.

I enjoy the simplicities and the freedom that they bring.

Your **truth** lies within…

Listen

and your *clarity* will spring forth,

Listen to your inner *guidance* and know your **truth**.

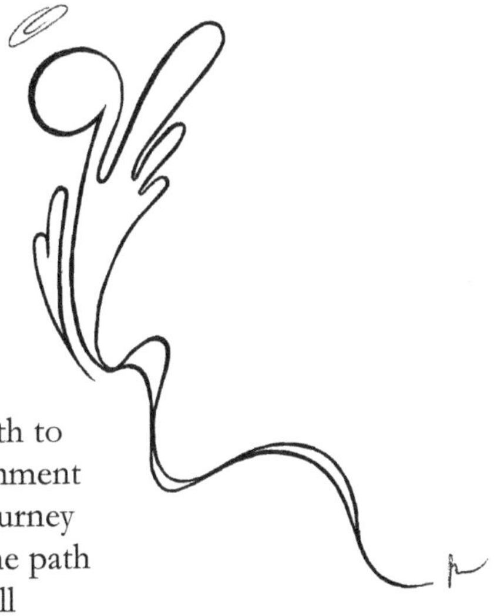

The path to enlightenment is the journey within, the path of all connectedness.

Life need not be complicated to be *Wonderful*.

Perfection in the imperfection

Simplicity
enough said.

There are times when I feel disappointment with others, that is when I need to love the most.

You would never have experienced the miracle of the silver lining if you had not found your way into the dark cloud.

Life is the ability to completely ***Feel***.

It is always a good idea to do a little spring cleaning, not just your home but your spirit and relationships, too.

That which you envision will be your reality.

Shift your perception and change your life.

Where there is *Hope* there is *Life.*

There is so much I don't know, every day I am gifted with a little more knowledge that wakes up the wisdom that lies deep within.

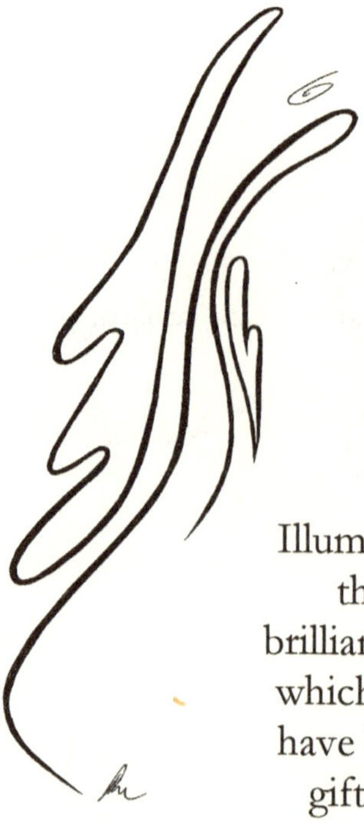

Illuminate the brilliance of which you have been gifted.

Listen to the *Whispers* in the *Wind.*

The World is
a Sea of Opportunity.
It is up to me to get my
feet wet.

Being a student makes for a great teacher.

To fill my hearts desires, I must first determine what they are.

Opportunities present themselves in times of abrupt changes.

Anything I am passionate about, I succeed in. This encourages me to try new things.

Fear is a choice; to be fearless is empowering.

As one door closes, another simultaneously opens...

Don't get stuck in the hallway.

Generosity and unconditionality are the solid foundation of an **Abundant Life**.

Some may call me a dreamer, I achieve many of my dreams.

I like to think that I am an achiever.

There is no lack in the universe, only narrow thinking.

Sometimes my greatest obstacles are my biggest blessings.

Vulnerability doesn't have to equate to weakness.

At times the only motivation I have is in knowing there is an end.

Only through introspection will you connect to the source and tap into the essence of your true self.

Introspection is the means of finding the answer to the timeless question, "Who am I?"

How you are is what you get.

What you do, how you think, the way you act, is what you will receive in life.

A clear intention at the start gives a more direct path.

It is important to be still from time to time, to allow movement to realign itself.

I realize great rewards when I give of myself, for that my life is very rich.

Choose wisely
as with every *choice* there come *Consequences.*

To make no choice ultimately leaves one adrift in a
Sea of Stagnation.

There is a magical realm inside each of us.

Only those who make the journey can truly know the gifts from within.

Wellness is a State of Mind

Through the **awakened** aspects of the **mind,** we achieve **Nirvana.**

Seeing past the **moment** to the bigger **picture.**

Alternative

Alter~Native

Sacred~Origins

Full Circle

We are One.

The more I **Embrace** my **Faith** the stronger it becomes.

~*Cycles*~

The power of the circle…

As it ends so it begins…

The perpetual Now…

Time waits for no one.

It is up to all of us
to connect with
the rhythmic melody
of the universe.

The awakened thought, the connected
heart, our soul source, we are one.

Only by the connection to the divine
source can we connect with each other.

Selfless Service
ultimately
serves self.

No matter how much
I give,
I receive
so much more.

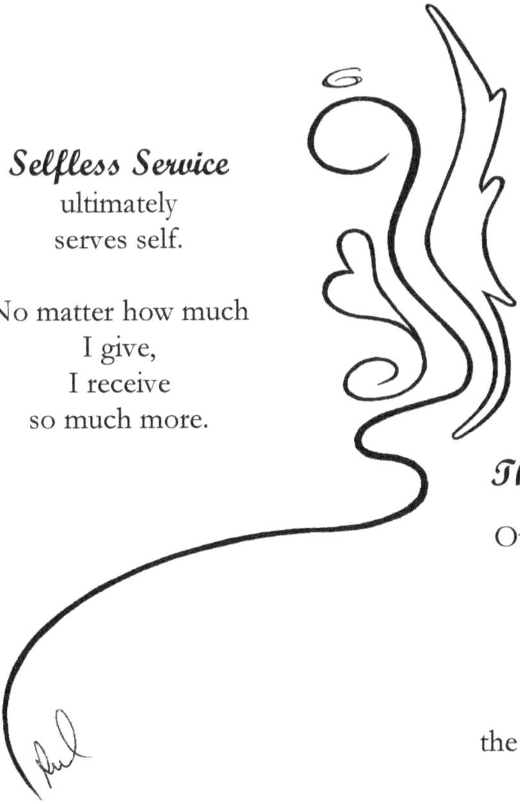

The Internal Drum

Our thoughts, our talk,
our walk,
all affect others.

Just as a drum
is able to receive
the resonance of another,
our hearts receive
what is around us.

Coming from
a place of Love…

Being true to Myself, my
Source, my Soul.

*The world is a
Beautiful Place!*

All things are
possible…

Believe in the
magic of your
dreams.

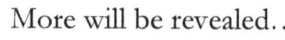

More will be revealed…

Free to be me.

Positive thinking,

Positive surroundings.

Peace is a concept of the heart, not the mind.

As the universe shifts, my energy changes.

I need to rethink my strategy of who I am evolving into.

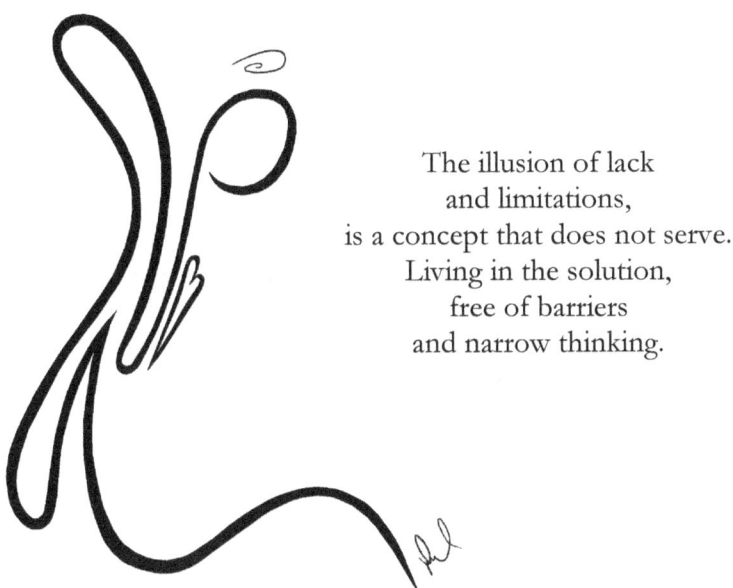

The illusion of lack
and limitations,
is a concept that does not serve.
Living in the solution,
free of barriers
and narrow thinking.

Change is inevitable; all roads lead home. Nothing truly is bad; it is just vibration and resonance.

To vibrate and sing is making music of the soul.

Harmonic balancing, singing, vibrating in a soulful melody, to be in grace with the divine.

Out of the Darkness and into the Light

Writing with my shadow hand, what am I to see?
Reveal to me my shadow side, what is there to be?
I am focused, I am clear,
Tell me, oh shadow, what does lie near?
My fears, my sadness, my doubts, my dread,
All lay below the shadow's head.
Rise to the surface, rise to the light,
No longer will I run in some exaggerated fright.
To the light I call you, surface, come now,
To the light I call you to heal somehow.
I faithfully wait, open and aware,
No longer will I allow, to be swayed or an easy scare.
Reveal to me, know my hidden truths,
Many lay dormant, as far back as my youth.
Rise to the surface, to light from above,
I will heal that which was hidden, with abundant pure love.
I will become whole with my fragmented self,
Back to what was intended, my wholeness, my health.
Here I sit with my shadow this day,
Awaiting the break, of the sun's morning ray.
To lighten up my shadow, my hidden, my fears,
That which I've run from, for most of my years.
To the surface I beckon, I've called to see,
Reveal to me now and so I'll set free.
Faithfully I sit, knowing somehow,
The layers of fears, will surface come now.
Come to the light, merge with the rest,
I'll know what I've feared and can become my true best.

Wholeness is what I've been intended from source,
Complete and beautiful, never my worst.
I've focused on that, which I've hidden away,
Most of my life, I couldn't see or wouldn't say.
Fearless and faithful, I've opened the lock,
My connection to source and know love is my rock.
Love is the answer, love is the way,
I'll heal completely now, starting this day.
I'm grateful and blessed, my truth what it is,
With faith for the love, my wholeness to witness.
As I heal, I will illuminate love,
For others to heal and connect with above.
I am to help, to serve, I know,
With guidance from source, I'll rely how to show.
No longer a prisoner of my own lock and key,
To the light my fears will soon be set free.
With love and faith I know in my heart,
We can all heal, in this unified start.

Healing is a process.

Healing is feelings, acceptance and faith.

Healing is a means of letting go.

I choose to lead today, not follow.
I choose to have a voice and no longer will be silent.
I choose today to take a stand, rather than to depend.
I've lacked confidence not ability.
I've lacked self-worth not caliber.

The time is *Now*.

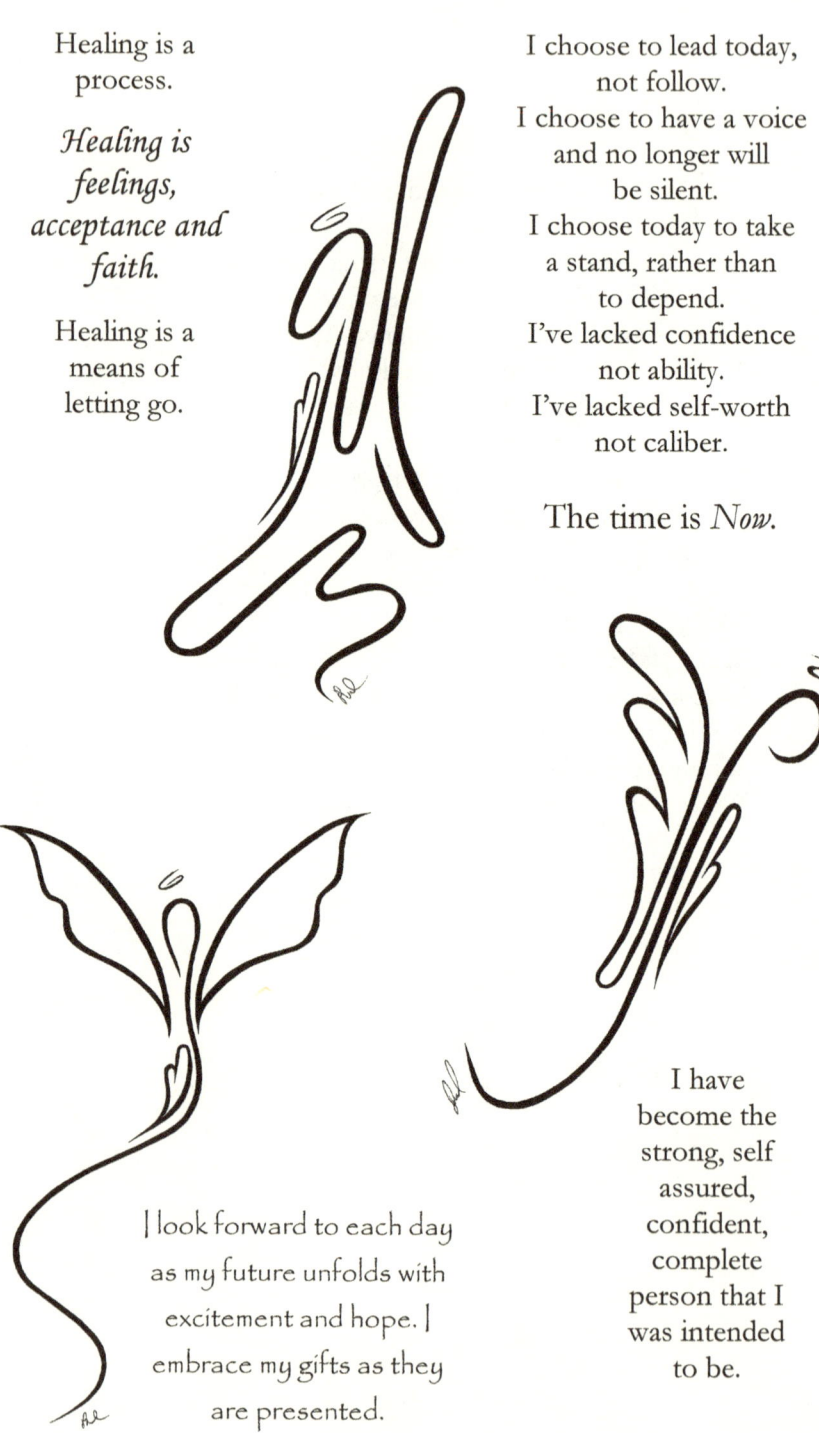

I look forward to each day as my future unfolds with excitement and hope. I embrace my gifts as they are presented.

I have become the strong, self assured, confident, complete person that I was intended to be.

Dreams have no boundary that is why I reach for the ***Stars***.

It is OK to help another fulfill their dreams as long as I don't sell out on my own.

As I ***Journey*** forward I invite only ***Love*** and ***Forgiveness*** for myself and for others. As I shift my thinking, so I shift my ***Life***.

~Transformation~
Change, movement, evolution…

This is a wondrous time to be alive.

What I focus on is what I invite into my life, which is why I reflect on my blessings with gratitude as often as I can.

I take great pride in knowing that I am a survivor, but that is no longer enough. Today I choose to live.

Lie-based thoughts are unrealistic and no longer welcome in my life.

I see only the best in people; I release any residuals of bitterness, resentment and fear. The love I have for others I clearly have for myself.

Reflections of the past build the gateway of tomorrow; only by knowing where you've been will you be able to know where you are going.

Being inspired and being able to find the joy in the simplicities of life. Knowing I need not participate in the chaos and drama by choice. Life always shows up; my perception of life is what creates the abundance of my blessings.

The physical world has a linear time frame that complicates your spiritual thinking.

No matter how dark the night may be, I trust completely that the sun will indeed rise.

Helping other people every day gives me hope.

Finding answers in the heart is the path I know towards faith.

Expect miracles and you'll be blessed beyond your wildest dreams.

I do things that make my heart sing, and yes, that is important.

I am as significant or as minute as a grain of sand, either way just as important.

Given the chance, people will reveal their true selves. Facades will fall, the veil of illusion will dissipate and our true essence will be revealed. Those who walk a path of honor will always shine.

Reflections of Us All

Shattered pictures on the wall,
Mirrored reflections cannot fall.
Upon the view, all eyes to see,
Is there anything whole that is left of me?
Looking past the facets within the mirror,
Why have I run most of my life in fear?
Fear no more, I will not run,
The past is the past, I accept it is done.
Here I stand quiet and still,
Allowing spirit to come and fill.
The emptiness within my soul awaits,
To fill the void with acceptance of fate.
I choose life, love, joy and bliss,
With positive intentions I cannot miss.
The Earth is changing and so must I,
As I let go of my past I'm able to fly.
Free my spirit, I spread my wings,
And now I know, my life can sing.
Freedom for all upon this New Earth,
As we assist her like she is giving birth.
To love, to nurture, it will take us all,
A unit of one, we cannot fall.
Together we can, together we must,
Open our hearts in a unified trust.
I know this is right, I am not alone,
The rebirth of the mother, the goddess, her throne.
With honor and respect, I humbly bow,
I ask for guidance, please just tell me how.
Together we unite, all the people as one,
Together we can, till the transformation is done.

Freedom in Letting Go

By letting and trusting in the wisdom of the divine plan will you be able to achieve your full potential.

Knowledge is Power

Ignorance is bliss, it has never really served. Break free of limitations and become open to opportunities and the possibilities. Shine like a beacon in the night, only then can you realize who you truly are.

Hold close to you that which you find dear.

Many teachers have crossed my path; I have gratitude for each and every one of them.

I choose to have people in my life who are loving and nurturing, who support my dreams.

Healing is shedding away the layers that do not serve and then filling that void in a loving divine way.

These are times of great change; much of what we have known to be true is no longer. Choosing what you value most will be the determining factor to the direction that your journey will take you.

Listen to your inner voice, it will not steer you wrong.

Divine guidance is available to all that ask, for all that open themselves to receive. Find time each day to quiet your world enough to hear.

Being **true** to myself….

Releasing that which does not serve.

Only by **letting go** will you be able to **Receive.**

To hold on longer than needed out of fear or obligation only restricts the ability to fully **realize** your **Greatness.**

Paradise is a State of Mind

Perception is key.

If you are not happy in the life you are living, experience it by changing the light.

Prioritizing my life…
Intentions make it so!

There is great value in each step we take. Free yourself from the mundane imprisonment you have accepted as your truth.

Settle for no less than your heart's desire.

Know you have great purpose and that what you are experiencing, and are to experience, are merely stepping stones along the way and each step making you a more complete person.

Many times in the course of life you will be put in a position that you will have to choose. Think with a clear mind. You are doing exactly what you are supposed to be doing right now.

The ultimate surrender is when you realize there is no right or wrong, then you will find peace along the way. Eventually we all end up at the same place. This journey we call life is truly what we make of it.

Connecting with spirit, acknowledging that all roads lead home.

Confidence

Truly believing in yourself.

To completely know yourself, free of all masks and facades. Oddly, there is a sense of security when you are stripped of your protective shields.

Know you have great purpose, what you are experiencing and are to experience are merely stepping stones along the way, each step making you a more complete person.

Many times in the course of life you will be out in a position that you will have to choose. Think with a clear mind; know you are doing exactly what you are supposed to be doing right now.

Make your choices wisely as they have a tendency to follow you.

Time is ever so precious...

Once it has gone, it can never be reclaimed. Memories are cherished moments of the past. To create the most wonderful memory is to immerse yourself in the experience as it is happening.

Embrace the moment, to be completely present.

Just because I go with the
flow doesn't mean I'm
not making conscious
choices in my life.

*I grow with each
accomplishment; there is
strength and power in
wisdom.*

Finding joy
when all you see
is darkness.
To help another
when you feel despair,
to call upon another when you
feel so alone,
the world is a better place.

Moments of Reflection

Sorting out my thoughts
embracing life
in its entirety,
feeling gratitude
for opportunities,
lessons and blessings.

What an
abundant life
I have!

I have realized that
I am stronger than
I know and I am
able to achieve
anything I set my
sights on.

Am I living or am
I existing?

Existence is
merely a default.

I Choose Life!

There are limitless
possibilities; I must be
free of doubt, which
locks the doorway to
my dreams.

*It is
necessary
for me to
participate
in my life.*

Abundance is here for us all.
We need to know, not
just believe.
Know it is available.
Don't ask why not - ask how!

*The future holds many
wondrous things...*

How it is, is how you create.

There is no lack in the
universe.
Relinquish all fear,
know and trust all is well.

How many times
I have shown up,
but not been
present.

A Time of Renewal....

I found a feather on the ground today,
On it placed a prayer then blew it away.
Off my hand I watched it,
Carried away by the breeze,
Knowing well my deepest wishes,
Soon to be received with ease.
Prayers and wishes, intended dreams,
Content my needs so well met,
My wants few or so it seems.
My prayers on a feather carried away,
I knew from the moment I woke,
This would be a special day.

As with any big storm, there is the **Promise** of a **Rainbow**.

It is in the stillness of my mind where my thoughts are the loudest. Almost like a distant song, ancient yet familiar, calling to me, a beaconing resonance of another time.

At some point in life, we all have to look in the mirror of Karma and see the reflection that each of us has created. Life is about choices and lessons to be learned. Numerous trails along the path have been laid and lessons can be learned in many ways.

If I am going to be a care giver, it just makes sense that I have something to give.

A new dawn, the day breaks - there is the wind of change.

Bliss is the radiance of your inner **Light**.

When I rid myself of toxins, I am free to flow with divine energies.

When that old doubt creeps in, it can just creep back out!

I am on a spiritual path, living in a physical material world.

I am clear and confident we are beyond our realm of comprehension and abundantly taken care of.

Positive Affirmations

Believing in myself because I know I can.

Doing so much better than I may be feeling, at times that I want to go into self-judgment.

Affirming my life, shifting my **Perception**.

Feelings can be distorted at times, I will not stuff them but allow them to pass through and be mindful that they are just temporary.

I choose to look at life as a rewarding experience. Even the "stuff" I think is bad, it's just life.

Reflections of the past...

To forgive is to relinquish ownership, thus freeing myself of bondage.

May I find the freedom I so request.

Embracing all that is wonderful in my life and consciously letting go of that which does not serve. Collectively, all my experiences have made me the person I am today. I choose to look at life as an adventure. Difficult times may come, but I try to embrace the lessons, not the drama. I love the person I have become and welcome life as it presents itself.

Love is what connects us to each other, the thread between the hearts of all humanity.

When we sever that connection, our spirit dies a slow death. We can reconnect at any time.

Sadness, depression and despair need not be our reality, but merely a temporary experience.

Reconnecting our hearts not only heals ourselves but heals us all.

It is time to realize my full potential.

I am open to new adventures and welcome prospects as they come to me.

The more I awaken I am able to see the path I am on is exactly where I need to be and I realize all is well.

No matter how wonderful my life is, I am still presented with challenges. The truth of my life is how I process and overcome those challenges.

You can't put a dollar sign on friendship, as love is priceless.

Some of my **greatest** accomplishments have been getting through the day without making things worse.

I have taken all of this far too serious, the key is in finding balance. If I am attempting to be on top of my game, I ask "shouldn't games be fun?"

With such multi-tasking lives, we need to remember to laugh. Playing and having fun should be part of our everyday routine, not a scheduled event once or twice a year.

The Gift of Awareness

I trust that in the midst of adversity there are blessings.

Though I have been on quite a complex journey, a labyrinth of life, I feel that there is a wondrous miracle in the making.

May each step bring joy, wisdom, health and freedom.

Acceptance on a Grander Scale

Traveling the straight and narrow is over-rated; there is a lot to be said for the twists and turns in life. Each turn has had hidden treasures and have been some of my most memorable moments. Sure, a straight path may be more direct and get you there quicker, but where is there and what's the rush anyhow?

Kindness, love, acceptance and respect, I wish for these. What I give, I open myself to receive.

My life is of my choosing, how I act is my choice.

I look at life much like a sunset. I can be moved by the panoramic view and the kaleidoscope of color, or get caught up in the impending darkness. Again I am reminded how precious each moment truly is and that life really is about choice.

When I am judging, I have found it usually is a reflection if myself. What I am trying to rid myself of is just what I am getting. Sometimes the greatest action is to be still.

Crystal Clear Intentions.

I feel a major shift happening. In the midst if the chatter I am trying to listen.

The nay-sayers serve no one.

As I rise above, I have clear thoughts and intentions.

I am free of unrealistic expectations. Sometimes I feel like I've missed the boat, but on the other hand, if I was supposed to be on that boat I would have been!

For years I had run from what I hold dear today.

I have always valued my independent thinking and my gratitude for not running with the pack.

~I Believe in Myself~

No matter what my past was or my perception of it, it is over. I only have today and a projection of a very bright future.

I have always danced to the beat of a different drummer, in the past I was a bit uncomfortable with that. Today I'm grateful I was able to dance.

I think everyone has a *take* on life and deserves to be heard. Do we need to be heard by *everyone*?

I feel confident about my future.

None of us are exempt. Life is a series of choices and consequences.

Living in the solution…

Guaranteed joy if that is your choosing.

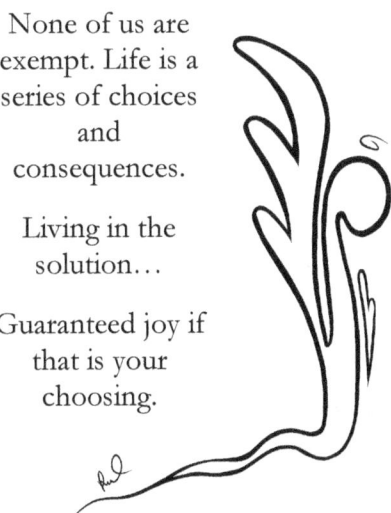

Ceremonial bonds, rites and rituals, power in unity, power in bonds. Like minds joining together in a common goal, to honor, to heal and to help heal. The nurturing spirit gathering in clan, how spirit brought us together, how spirit assists us on our journey. From such diverse worlds in which we come, together again, bonding in love, uniting in goals, driven by spirit. Kindred souls searching, looking for our truth and knowing the unknown as spirit directs, as our awareness grows. Together in spirit, together again, each of us with our own special gifts and with the knowledge to share as we receive, we are able to achieve another level of wholeness, to nurture, to love, to heal and to celebrate. We are experiencing change, each doing our own part in destiny, and are aware of the changes that must take place. To find our way to the place that we can each give of ourselves in the rebirthing process. We follow our hearts, trust our intuitions accept the signs and respond as we are guided. At one in our group, just a segment of a much larger, more diverse clan, knowing our participation is necessary if we are going to survive our human condition. To continue to aide in the healing of our beloved Mother Earth, the goddess from which we were all born, and to honor her and all of our existences as sacred, beautiful creations. We are now coming full circle. As we experience the moment it is gone and a new one is born. With transformation, growth and acceptance, I participate with love in my heart and spirit guiding my soul. I sit here with the others honoring the changes and willing to use my energy to aide in the process. Fall is upon us and as we enter into a dormant time we rest, charged and prepared for spring. We will need our strength to continue the birthing process. Honor our collective power in the clan to lead the way when it is time. Shared love and energy, we all grow as we give and receive of each other. I hold my arms stretched out and take the hand of another to lead and to be guided, we are already here. The time has come to be open, participate in the exchange as a necessary act. It is imperative we listen, look for the signs and follow as spirit guides us. It is darkest before the dawn; it is time for us all. As I embrace the energies and look to the universe, grateful for my existence, I say with love, blessed be.

The Tides of Change...

Moving forward, I secure
solid ground
during these times of
transition.

I am surrounded by Love.

**The
opportunity
to realize
my truth.**

Living in the Solution

Time to be
Time to heal
Time to love

I have joy in my heart,
I live a grand life.

I must not
get too
attached to
the daily
drama.

The Future Feels Good!

I am taking time to be quiet and listen.

As I heal, I am able to make sound choices of what I want to invite into my life.

Peace and Love
That is all that really matters.

There are so many people in my life; loneliness comes from lack of intimacy. I get lonely, though I am seldom alone. I have built walls to protect myself, now I have realized they have left me alone, floating in an abyss. Walls to protect my heart from being hurt, but separation is so much worse. Pain is a great motivator.

I don't stop reaching out just because others don't reach back. There are times I wonder what I am reaching for?

To keep moving forward, speed or distance does not matter, it is about the direction. I believe that good direction will get me where I want to go, I don't really want to go too quickly; I wouldn't want to miss a thing. The key is to just keep moving.

The Future is Bright!

Being here, in existence during these changing times, is truly a momentous experience.

We are our dreams;
in the darkness and slumber
the truth awakens.

We are excelling beyond our current comprehension.

Chapter Three

A Whisper of Love

Dreams

Finding truth in the threads of our dreams is what gives us the strength to keep pushing on.

I have had so much fear and judgment in my life that it had crippled me at times. I have reached a point in my life where I am taking a stand and with as much strength as I can gather I say, "Why not me?" Great things happen for great people, or so I had always been taught. What I believe is that great things happen for people who believe; again I say, "Why not me?" I look back over my life and my heroes have always been the ones with determination, focus and a strong belief in self. Not one of my heroes have ever been born of opportunity or privilege. Not that there is anything wrong with any station we are born to, but I find it important that I can relate to certain similarities to help me squash that built-in saboteur who plays games with my dreams. Who I was and where I came from should not be the defining criteria of who I am today or what I aspire to do in my life. Limitations are those that I self-impose, again, "Why not me?" Every person I have labeled as great has seen their share of adversity and failure. I look to that as motivation and strength rather than defeat or my ticket to give up. I am living a life of my dreams, a life I had read about in story books as a child, which at the time I had looked at my life with shame. I am able to say that I can now proudly look back at those experiences as they were the driving forces for me to not want more, but to want better. I have learned along this journey called life that more is simply that, just more. Better is about change and it is up to me as to what I am to change and I hope that as I better myself, I better the lives of those around me. "Why not me" has been a driving force in my life for some time now and I can only hope it continues as it serves me well.

more from spirit...

Hum a tune today,
even if it is the blues.
You are a composer
with a work in
progress.

Don't get caught in the illusion of the physical; it isn't real. Trust your inner guidance as it will not steer you wrong. Your inner vision knows the truth.

Try to make each day
Special
as it is ***unique***
on its own.

Some times we don't realize how much of ourselves we have given away until we get it back.

To be able to learn from our challenges and seeing a positive outcome in the midst of adversity is such a gift.

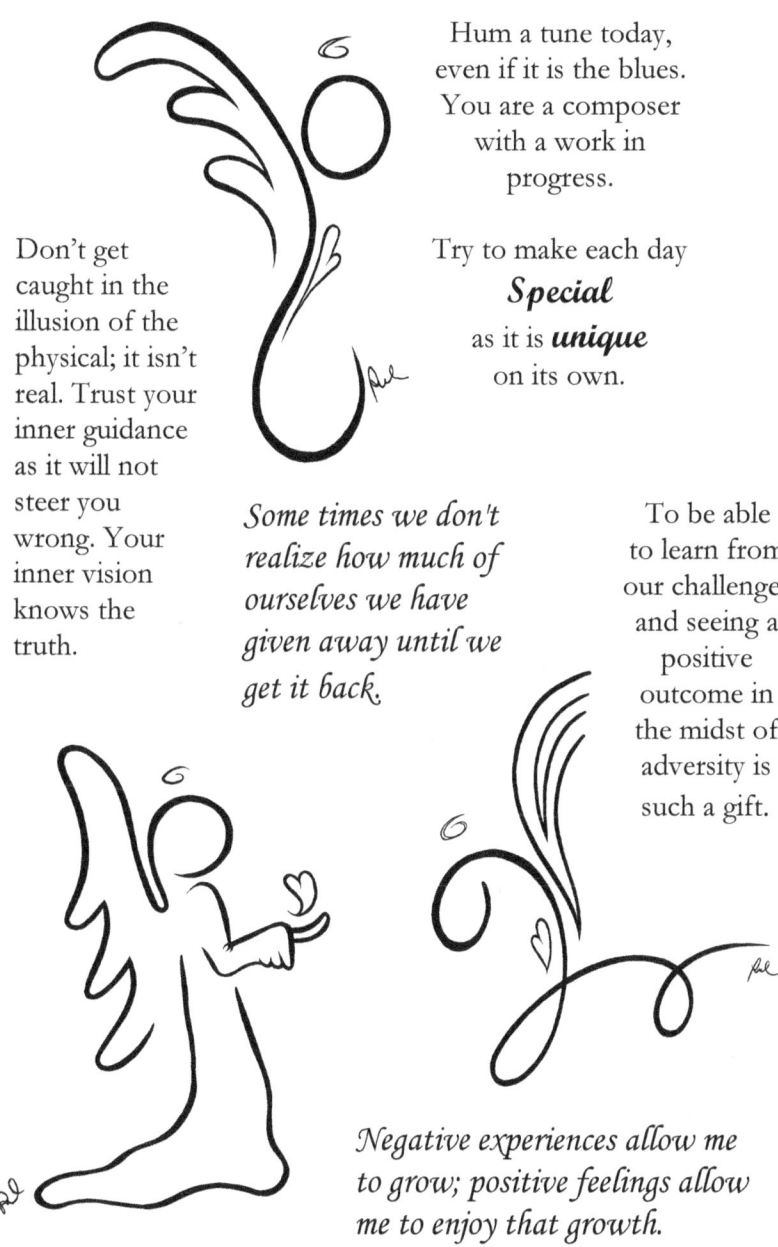

Negative experiences allow me to grow; positive feelings allow me to enjoy that growth.

To know myself, my inner truth, to realize my full potential, I am confident in my decisions and free of attachments. I am becoming whole maybe for the first time.

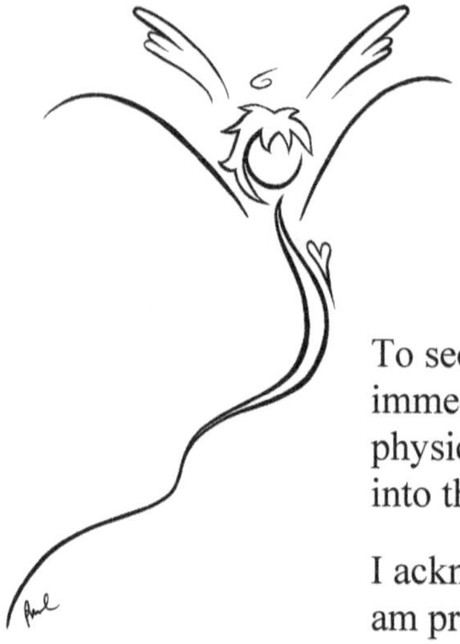

Free from the self-made bondage of judgment and fear. Free to be authentic, free to be me.

To see past the immediate, the physical and dive into the abyss.

I acknowledge that I am protected, guided and will find the energy to carry on.

One can not always assume.
One must be aware,
knowledgeable and take action!

It has become very clear that it isn't all about me. When I look at life in this manner, it makes for a wonderfully positive perspective on a seemingly mundane existence.

I embrace the loving, generous selfless nature in which I try to live my life. I must be careful as to not over compensate and loose me in the process.

I have come to realize some of my heaviest burdens are from that which never was.

People we meet on our journey are merely stimuli in which we can look inside of ourselves and retrieve the spiritual awakening we have been searching for.

𝒫eace of 𝒨ind - I choose to keep it today.

I know my little bit does make a difference.

To love myself is to love all of me, to accept the good and the bad.

To let go of something deeply rooted is going to leave a wound. I must allow myself to heal and acknowledge my vulnerability.

Even in the darkest of times, there is light. In the shadows you learn your truth. In the stillness awaken and listen, within the subtle whispers you will hear.

Maybe I needed to hit that brick wall to wake me up, bricks of love and mortar of light.

Life is a series of steps that go in whatever direction you choose. It is amazing that a series of bad choices along the way can turn into an avalanche without any warning. Perhaps it could have been avoided if only I were awake.

Dance to the Light of the Rainbow

The way of the light bearer, to walk a straight path,
Dance the light of the rainbow, only love will de-spell the wrath.
The magic of ages, the way as it has been told,
Is there for all, for the meek and the bold.
Walk the straight path, and dance to the rhythm of the rainbow light,
Dance to the melody, till time adjusts and is set right.
A manifestation of projection, fears and blessings, too,
The world will recreate with a blueprint made by you.
There are those running to their demons created by themselves,
Hold close what you find dear, embrace love as you near the Twelves.
Circle in bands, as the masses unite,
The planet now off kilter, soon to be set right.
The choice is yours, the path to be free
Always love is the answer, know love is the key.

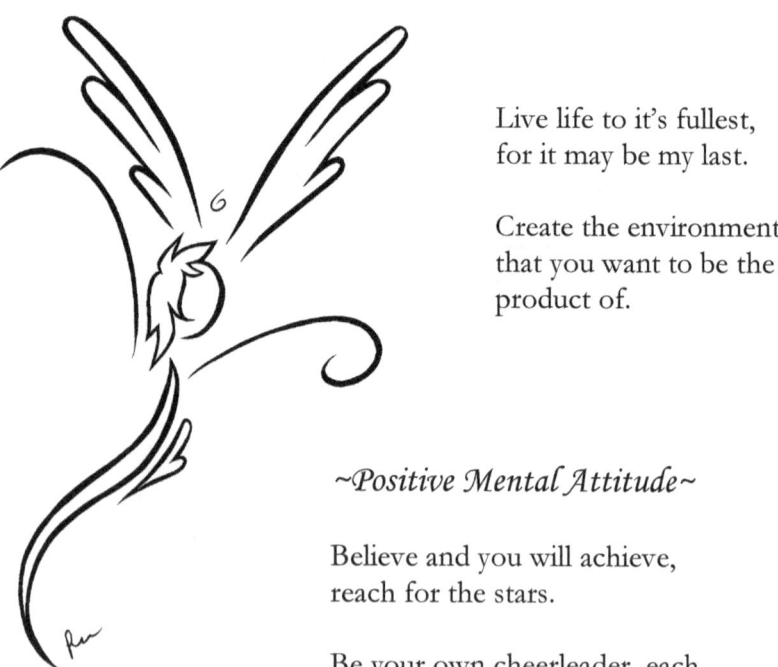

Live life to it's fullest, for it may be my last.

Create the environment that you want to be the product of.

~Positive Mental Attitude~

Believe and you will achieve, reach for the stars.

Be your own cheerleader, each step is a journey in its' self.

For years I ran from my dark side, the truth is I ran from my light.

Only when I realized how spiritually bankrupt I was, living in a black hole of my own digging, was I able to stop the process and begin to experience the miracle called life.

State the obvious and be open for change, know the truth lies within.

Dispense the fear with light, you are stronger than you know.

Be aware of your thoughts as they create your reality. You are what you think, you feel what you think. Think your way into a good way of life.

I try to own up to my mistakes, to see what I have done and to look forward.

I trust that there is purpose for who I am and what I do.

Trust the knowing you have, your intuition is the wisdom you must rely upon.

Happiness is a state of mind, not a place to be. I've come to realize with my collective wisdom that you don't acquire, you achieve, and the only way you achieve is to do the footwork.

To achieve happiness is to achieve inner peace.

Adversity, *what a wonderful lesson to learn and to grow from.*

I love not only my accomplishments and talents, but my vulnerable side as well.

Smoother roads ahead, the worst is behind me. I have achieved and see progress. Something has shifted and I will continue to implement change in a positive way. My focus is clearer and I am making good decisions.

~Believing in Miracles~

You are special
beyond your knowing and soon
will become aware.

It is dawn, the beginning of a new day.

To make a decision I must be in full agreement and aligned. It has been my experience that if my head, my heart and my gut are not in alignment, I do not act and the answer is no.

Life is one big lesson and time seems to be part of an illusion; we just have to be.

All days are good if I look at them with love and acceptance.

I try to look at the whole picture, not just a frame at a time.

There is nothing wrong with being a work in progress.

I've walked in faith though at times it may have been blind; I have never lost sight of my dreams. Sometimes the indirect path is the one to take.

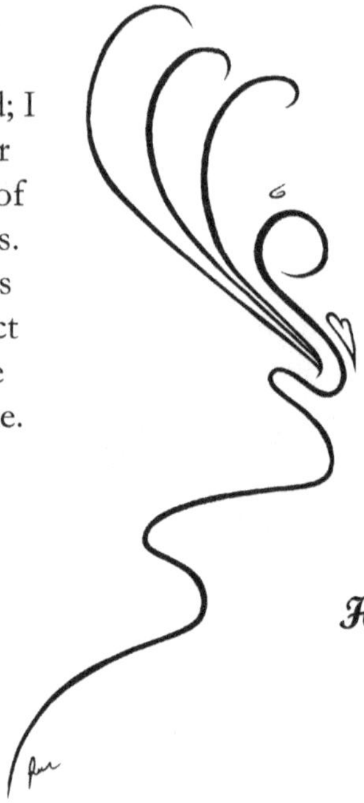

I believe people are a product of their choices. I too have made poor choices in my past, but I believe I've redeemed myself on some level and the choices I am making today are not only good for me, but for the betterment of us all.

Hidden Blessings…

Adventures in a *New Day.*

New Beginnings…

You're never alone in friendship.

$\mathcal{L}$ife…I know when I run from me it just gets worse. When I choose to be still and participate in my life, it always seems to just work out.

If I am on a quest for acceptance and unconditional love, I must be enmeshed in some form of judgment.

I need to focus on where the extremes of my personality intersect. That is when a healing can take place, in the neutral zone where darkness meets the light.

~See the Beauty in all Things~

Forgiveness
is the ability
to give
Love.

Be aware of the subtle nudges as they are guidance that you seek.

Only in the still of your aloneness will you become one.

Much of my life I had lived in fear, doubt and lack. Those were lessons to make me strong, to make me realize my worth. Only when beaten can you realize the depth of your strength and quality. Only in the darkness of adversity can you truly see the light.

If I am well I can take care of others, if I am whole I can show up in my life, if I am secure I can be of service.

When I take care of myself, I seem to do better with the rest of my life.

Finding Perfection in Where I Fit

There is a sense of grace when the wind blows through the trees, the one-leggeds, or ancient ones as some call, with broken beams of light finding their way through the canopy overhead as I walk along a virgin path. The road less taken is a phrase I hold dear to my heart as my feet find their way on the ground below. I walk a path of my own making, confident when I am among my tall friends. I have a sense of belonging that seems so foreign when I am with my kind, perhaps that is a key.

Outward appearances should not dictate what my kind is, my inner vibration the resonance of my heart in harmony when I am truly with my kind. It is sad to me the mass judgment the human race has as a result of our physical coverings. For years being a square peg trying to fit into a round hole, it never did it occur to me that the hole was the wrong shape. My truth on this Earth walk is to find perfection in where I fit.

I am open to
receive the
guidance that I
am asking for.

I will not limit myself.

I realize that the musts in
life are also choices. Today
I choose wisely and make a
conscious effort to bring
joy to others.

I continue to look at life as a series of
opportunities; it is up to me to rise to the
occasion as it is presented. There is
worth in what I do; may I continue to
make a difference.

I'm not merely trying; I'm actually doing and just waiting for the feelings to catch up.

Of my many gifts I am especially fond of the gift of awareness.

To realize that I only have now, there are no more tomorrows, only todays.

I may not know where I am going, but I am confident that I am on the right path.

I know I am a work in progress and I choose to change, not from me but into me.

Awakening to my Life's Purpose

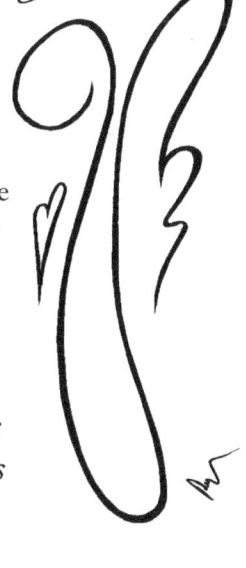

It is much easier to see the bigger picture when I'm not in the middle of it.

I choose activities that support my intentions.

Life is a roller coaster of experiences. It is up to me as to whether they are scary or exciting.

As much as I know the journey of self realization is an inside job, I know I can't do it alone.

I believe the world waits with open arms.

The belief you hold is what maps out your journey.

I have found great satisfaction in doing a life review. I've had some really good times, some very hard times, but more than anything the enjoyment of reclaiming me.

A small act of kindness can go a long way.

Though I am a work in progress it is important that I focus on my accomplishments, not my shortcomings.

Listen to nature, it is through the subtle messages that you will hear.

Being human is not a sentence.

Being available and present is a gift. Life is an adventure and the possibilities are endless.

I look at the people I surround myself with; I feel this is a clear indication of where I am. Do I judge or criticize, am I indifferent or do I truly care and express unconditional love? They are my mirror of how I think of myself at any given time.

What a gift it is to be able to fully experience a second chance. I have made peace with myself, and no longer choose fear as my traveling companion. It seems that when I give myself a break and quit being a victim or prisoner of my ego I do so much better. Amazing the freedom I get from self through acceptance.

Answers come to all of my questions though they may not be what I had expected. Perhaps it isn't the answer I need to be asking for but rather the questions.

Being different has separated me much of my life. I have come to a place of acceptance that different isn't bad, it makes me special and I enjoy being unique. My qualities and who I am bring me joy today. I love the person I have become and I am able to radiate that love to others.

When you tell yourself something long enough you'll start to believe it. Today I affirm my existence and realize that self-attack keeps me down. Constructive criticism doesn't work if you are the one dishing it out.

When the clouds of uncertainty rain on my path, I put up the umbrella of faith to protect along the way.

I have finally allowed myself to become vulnerable and have allowed others to see the real me. What I found is the real me was a person I had never met.

I embrace all of the goodness that the universe has to offer. I choose to be free of all attachments that are limiting and hold me back from my full potential.

There are times that I am a deep thinker and have been known to get lost in my thoughts. If I don't do anything with them, they are no more than clutter in my head.

The paralyzing aspect of fear has brought me to my knees more times than I am willing to admit. What better place is there than that to be humbly calling out for help?

Choose wisely, as with every choice there are consequences. Know that the best choice may not be the easiest or the most popular.

Each of us has had memorable times that mark milestones or present a turning point and these don't have to be big events. One of my most significant came when I was at an intersection waiting for the light to turn. I looked out the window and there on the median was a dusting of purple flowers, called weeds by most I am sure. I wondered how many had sat at that exact spot waiting and never noticed the magnificence that was right there beside them?

May the blessings of your light illuminate so others may find their way. May the beauty of your gifts bring joy to another.

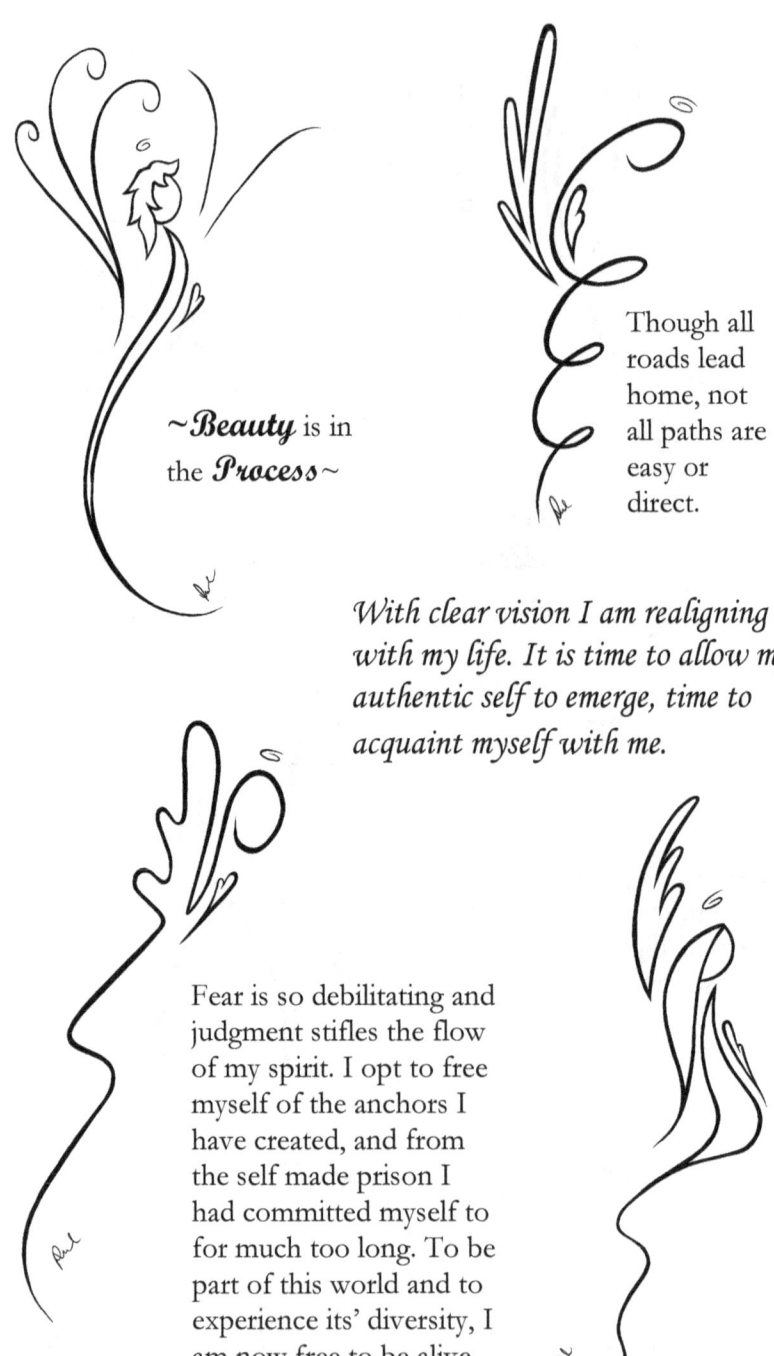

~*Beauty* is in the *Process*~

Though all roads lead home, not all paths are easy or direct.

With clear vision I am realigning with my life. It is time to allow my authentic self to emerge, time to acquaint myself with me.

Fear is so debilitating and judgment stifles the flow of my spirit. I opt to free myself of the anchors I have created, and from the self made prison I had committed myself to for much too long. To be part of this world and to experience its' diversity, I am now free to be alive.

Through the obstacles of life, I seek knowledge, truth and peace.

As life presents itself, I try to be aware of the blessings each experience has brought me.

The phrase "perception is key" keeps surfacing in my life. In business, marketing and labeling make all the difference. Abstract art gets so much merit but distorted thinking is frowned upon. I wonder, is there really any difference?

I no longer hold onto relationships out of obligation. The relationship that needs the most nurturing is the one with me.

In the stillness of your mind you receive the guidance that you seek.

I am becoming more aware of my blessings.

Listen to the rhythms; observe that which you see, not only with your physical eyes, but with your inner vision as well.

As I emerge into darkness, to an eclipse of my soul, I ask, "what is there that needs illuminated?"

My hidden truth, what is it that I have not been able to see?

We learn many lessons from our teachers and then we teach them to be even better.

I know and trust that my truth is what it is, and I don't need to explain myself. To be selfish at times is giving a gift to one's self.

When my head, my heart and my gut are in alignment, I know that I am on the right path.

I am dancing to the rhythm of the universe; occasionally it changes beat.

I want to participate but sometimes I need to step aside, watch the choreography to learn the steps.

I am clear that I don't have to have all of the answers and I have become aware that it isn't necessary that I have all of the questions.

When I am feeling kicked to the curb, I need to look at who is doing the kicking. Much to my surprise it usually is me!

I need to keep doing all of the things that keep me centered even if I don't get immediate results.

As I rise to the occasion, I try to be in the solution and to be present in my life. I am beginning to realize my value and embrace it. My life has been quite the journey as I seek out my truth; all is well if I choose to see it that way.

How is it that I have become so accomplished in my life, but fail to see that as I fall back into fear and doubt?

How we are, really is about awareness and choice.

Of all the inspirational books, talks and seminars that I've had the opportunity to experience, I've been most impacted by the voice within.

Though it may be familiar, if it no longer works it is not acceptable.

I grow when I help others. Peace and love are my motivation. A shift in perception, it really is a choice. What actually changes and how does it happen?

Only when I can love myself, I can love another. To continually give and not allow yourself to receive makes you imbalanced.

One must have Balance to have Peace.

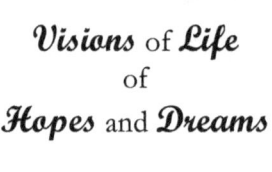

Visions of *Life*
of
Hopes and *Dreams*

I am living a
Life Beyond
expression!

Taking one step at a time to achieve my dream…

Sure of my direction, confident in the guidance I have been gifted.

I have come to a place where I truly appreciate myself.

I connect with my life, all of it.

As I look at the bigger picture, nothing has ever been as it had initially appeared.

Letting go is never easy.
May our hearts be warmed with memories of joyous times. May we sing in a loved filled manner and may the gardens of our soul all know Eden.

Loneliness is a state of mind not a state of being. We are never truly alone if we have an open heart.

May
Peace and
Love
Prevail

There is no past as the future waits.

I am constantly aware of this moment, the knowing that this place in time, now, is all that truly exists.

As the sun rises, it brings about a new set of experiences and lessons. As I awaken, my being has been renewed and my perception recaptured.

Chasing your dream,
Dream big,
Magic of your dreams,
Dreams do come true.

The journey in fulfilling a dream can be filled with the unexpected and surprise. On occasion I found my dream was merely a doorway to an experience I didn't even know I wanted, only to realize it was exactly what I had been missing all along.

Even when I am standing still, quiet in my space there is movement.

Just as the sun rises so the day begins, the cycle of life to which we all belong.

There are many seasons in our lives, each bring their own gifts and lessons. There seems to be a natural cycle, and as I look back, I can clearly see the springs, falls and winters of my life. The one I enjoy the most is spring; it is the time to wake from a long winter's nap, hibernation and introspection. In spring I come alive once again, ready to bring forth the next level of newness into my life. Spring is the adventure, the unknown, like a blank canvas and I am the pallet of paint ready to co-create.

I need to believe that there is a reason and a purpose for the experiences I have in my life. The truth lies within my heart, through a quiet introspection I can more clearly see.

There truly is no loss, only change.

Nobody wins when you cloud your heart. To make a difference, some times the smallest gestures are more than enough. That is more than most of us can ever hope for, to just have enough.

No more time for indifference, I must take a stand.

Knowledge is the key, knowledge is freedom, and wisdom is the way out.

Illumination starts from within.

Into the depths of my subconscious lays an aspect of fear, solidified and reinforced over time. Understanding the innocence of its quality, I must love and forgive, ultimately that is the key.

Trust that you really do know more than you think. Speak your truth with kindness; listen to your thoughts with love in your heart.

Look towards the outcome, projection to the end result will speed up the process. Look forward. Don't focus too long on where you are or you will grow roots. Take note of where you presently stand and use that to obtain direction. Look at each step, but maintain your focus to the end.

Like attracts like, not a new concept, but one I try to live by. What I put out is what I am inviting into my life. I have learned through my life experiences that awareness and conscious choices make my world a beautiful place.

The time is now....

I welcome the end of prosperity and all attachments to greed, fear and ego.

The beginning of abundance, security in knowing there is more than enough. What a relief to be able to exhale. Trust the source is limitless.

Something happens with age. At some point if we don't fight it we mellow. Knowledge turns to wisdom and our drive changes, it seems more focused. Like a wondrous stew on a winter's night.

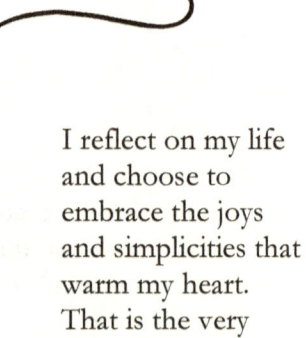

This experience we call life is a constant moving entity and we must allow ourselves to enjoy the ride.

I reflect on my life and choose to embrace the joys and simplicities that warm my heart. That is the very same heart that allows me to love and to be loved.

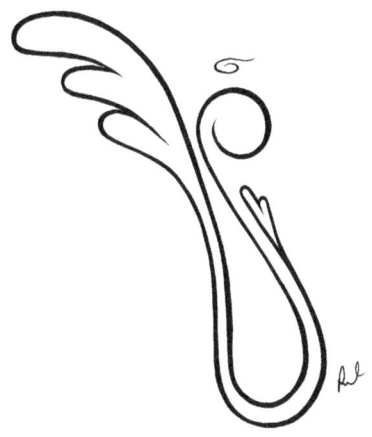

My circle of life is what it is right now. I try to find balance with a sense of humor, and not take any of it too seriously. Life is a series of experiences and lessons; I need to take them as such. Free myself of any attachments, those attachments that solidify and emotions that inhibit movement, flow and growth. Constant movement is the key, movement with intent.

Hold strong during the winds of change. They are not meant to blow you down, rather to cleanse you deeply from that which has imprisoned you like a cocoon of darkness.

To be a team player, together we are one. There is power in the unification, much greater than just the sum total. Together the collective we, working as one can make all the difference.

As I release my fears, some that have been with me for many years, I embrace the lessons they have brought to strengthen and empower me.

It is even more vital that I look at my assets and what is going right in my life rather than put all of my energy on where I'm falling short.

Direct may be the quickest, however, to experience a wondrous journey there must be some twists and turns.

Life is great when I'm actually living it.

It usually isn't what I'm doing, but what I'm not doing that speaks volumes.

At some point you stop running and at that moment you get a glimpse of who you were always meant to be.

Though I have always danced to the beat of a different drummer I wasn't alone, I just hadn't yet met the others.

Self-worth, Self-confidence, Self-reliance, I am so much more than I give myself credit for.

~Breaking Free~

Just because things have always been a particular way does not mean I can't change at any time. Life should be free-flowing. I believe in myself more each time I take action. Today the validation I need comes from within. The more I direct my focus inward, the stronger I become.

When I shift my perception, I don't care any less about you but care more about me.

We all have the ability to make our worlds that which we desire. We are what we believe, what we desire, what we choose. We are here to help each other and by that we help ourselves.

I have awakened to my presence, I am now recognizing the others and together we are able to make a difference.

I am becoming increasingly aware that we as people are all the same. Our outward appearances may differ, but the essence of who we are is amazingly similar.

There are times I feel so confused and at the blink of an eye everything is all so clear. I know I must continue to trust, to make choices with pure intentions, to truly believe my life has significance.

I have been able to realize there is wisdom in all of my experiences if I look at the larger picture. When I stop fragmenting my life and take off the self imposed blinders, I can usually see the solution quite clearly.

I have peace in my heart and joy in my life. To truly know serenity, I need it not to be merely glimpses but an integral part of my life.

I am no longer willing to settle. Why lower my standard of excellence when I know I deserve only the best?

There is a purpose for all I see and do, and to know fully my needs are and will always be met.

Acceptance and unconditional love are so empowering. When I free myself from expectations, I find relief and peace as I let go.

Open your hearts completely, only then will you be able to freely and abundantly receive. By giving you create a vacuum. Letting go of toxins and limiting attachments you soften your heart. By giving with love you receive so much more.

Life really is what you make of it. If I can accept and appreciate what I get without condition and not create havoc, I'm actually doing pretty well. It is so much easier to come from a place of love than to be judgmental. When I come from love I feel free.

When my head becomes consumed with a spin of negativity, I am prepared with empowering mantras and affirmations to shift myself back on to a positive course.

Thoughts are as powerful as our actions, be mindful of what you project. What you put out will be returned to you and then some. I am not able to entertain more than one thought at a time

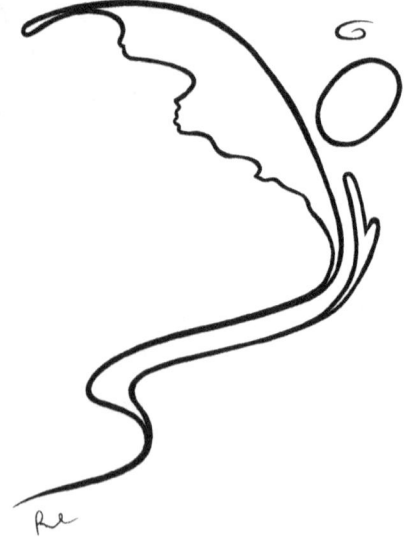

What counts is my being, my thoughts, my dreams and my desires. I am special and have to give myself permission to feel and express them.

I have always felt that we are the captain of our ship and spirit is the propulsion, we must choose direction and move. Stagnation encourages disease, movement without direction encourages chaos, direction without guidance is shear self-will. A good life maintains connection, balance, focus and love.

The answer is always with love. As I prioritize my life, really looking at what is important, all those secondary attachments seem to fall away.

More isn't always better; sometimes I get lost in a sea of life. Simplicity and a fresh look at joy, what am I inviting into my life? What I surround myself with is what I become.

If I am not at peace with me, I'll never be at peace in the world.

Emotional pain is temporary and exists as long as I choose to hold on to it.

Once I have accepted that I deserve, I find that I have opened a door in which to receive.

Everything is temporary...
As I move forward fearlessly, I am aware that my experiences come with lessons and I grow as a result of each of them.

I've always felt that I was on this planet to help others; I just never realized I needed to help and heal me first.

I know I don't need to have validation from outside sources to make me a person, but it sure makes it easier and helps my confidence to have support.

Sometimes you need to go back in order to go forward.

I learn and so I teach; I am taught and so I learn.

I feel like I am waking up for the very first time, what an exciting experience.

I embrace the joy I have been given and try to be generous with it.

Like colors of the rainbow, we are all different and needed to make the whole, but that doesn't mean we are all going to blend well.

I think the journey truly is the destination and with each step I want to be aware. I don't want to be so busy that I miss all I've been looking for. To look and digest the scenery, to embrace each moment before I move onto the next. Not only do I have hope, but I have direction.

For much of my life I have been giving away my personal power; with new found awareness, I am taking it back.

My best is good enough; I'm not settling but accepting.

I feel the people in my life are not there by chance. There is a well orchestrated chain of events that has brought us all together.

Life is an initiation; life is a dance, choreography of invitation and response. Each step we take with our feet upon the earth is like the beat of a drum, sending a message of resonance to everyone and everything and in return we receive and internalize all that is sent to us. Choose wisely as that which you send out will come back to you.

Focus on that which you desire, that which fuels your dream. Create your life so that you live that dream.

The world is a gift and I am now seeing glimpses of the bigger picture. When I let go of those limiting anchoring beliefs, I find that I am free to see the life of my choosing. Today I am living in paradise.

I need to just be sometimes to experience and to enjoy. When I'm doing that, I refuel myself. It has always been difficult for me to just relax, I have a tape that plays in my head that tells me that being idle is bad, that rest is lazy and if I'm not moving I am stagnant and will begin to rot. That tape needs to be reprogrammed. I may not be physically moving, but there is clearly movement, spiritually and emotionally; refueling more rapidly when I am still.

I no longer have the luxury to blame another. There is a place where truth meets the soul and thought; it may be different than what I had anticipated, though wonderful in union.

Everything is temporary. Grab all that you can, touch as many hearts as you are able along the way and share love.

I know I need to embrace the world without fear or judgment. With acceptance and unconditional love, I know my journey will take me to wonderful places.

A time of completion, the end marks the beginning and the start of a new cycle. As I find my way, may I choose wisely, moving towards a future free of drama, free to be me, my authentic self, free to be.

Living my life is so much more exciting than worrying about it and all that I have allowed to paralyze me. I am no longer anchored to my past because I chose to let go of it. There is so much beauty that lies ahead; I don't want to miss a thing!

The feeling of accomplishment is achieved when a project has found its way to the end; it isn't anything that can be purchased or gifted. This is something that must be obtained by perseverance, vigilance and a belief in one's self. I had been taught to express myself in whatever media I was working with as if it were for me alone. Something generic happens to art and the artist when a dollar sign is attached. I am not to say that is a bad thing, we live in a materialistic world and all need to have our obligations met; however, for the unseasoned it is best to be driven by shear desire, not financial outcome. It has been my experience that the end result of my best work has been produced in that manner.

www.ingramcontent.com/pod-product-compliance
Lightning Source LLC
Chambersburg PA
CBHW020012050426
42450CB00005B/438